The Smallest Life Around Us

Exploring the Invisible World of Microbes with Eight Easy At-Home Experiments

BY LUCIA ANDERSON · ILLUSTRATED BY LEIGH GRANT

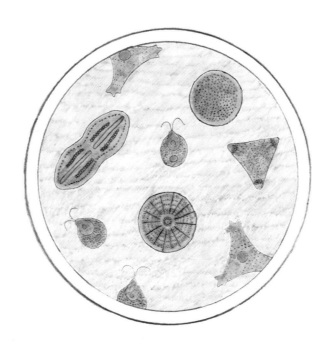

CROWN PUBLISHERS, INC., NEW YORK

Text copyright © 1978 by Lucia Anderson
Illustrations copyright © 1978 by Leigh Grant

Published by Crown Publishers, Inc., 225 Park Avenue South, New York,
New York 10003 and represented in Canada by the Canadian MANDA Group
CROWN is a trademark of Crown Publishers, Inc.
Manufactured in Hong Kong
Library of Congress Cataloging-in-Publication Data
Anderson, Lucia.   The smallest life around us.   Summary: A brief discussion of one-celled plants and animals
known as microbes. Suggested experiments are included. 1. Micro-organisms—Juvenile literature.
[1. Micro-organisms] I. Grant, Leigh. II. Title.   QR57.A48   576   77-15858
ISBN 0-517-53227-1
ISBN 0-517-56549-8 (pbk.)
10 9 8 7 6 5 4 3

 **To Silas**

Tiny plants and animals live all around us. We cannot see them because they are so small, but they are everyplace.

They live in the soil, the air, and in rivers and oceans. They
grow on the highest mountains and in the deepest caves. Some live in
the ice at the north and south poles; some live where it is very hot.
They are found throughout cities and in the country. They grow on
other plants and animals. Some are even living on you, on your skin,
hair, and inside your body, in your mouth, nose, and all through
your intestines.

These tiny plants and animals are called *microbes*. The word microbe is made from two other words: *micro*, meaning small, and *bios*, meaning life. So, microbe means small life.

Microbes have been on earth for a very long time. They may have been the first forms of life to exist. Today there are more microbes in the world than all other living things.

For thousands of years people did not know microbes existed.
They were too small for them to see.

But people did see many changes in their world—important
changes. And they did not know what caused them. They saw food
that they kept too long change color and begin to smell bad. They saw
cuts and wounds grow red and sore and become infected. They saw
old plants and leaves and trees crumble apart on the forest floor and
disappear into the soil. Such changes were a natural part of the world,
but people did not understand them. They did not know these changes
were evidence of tiny plants and animals growing all around them.

About three hundred years ago, a Dutch lensmaker named Anton Van Leeuwenhoek was the first person to see microbes. In 1676 he made magnifying lenses and used them to look at common things around him. When he looked at pond water, he discovered that in just one drop a world of tiny wiggling creatures existed. Van Leeuwenhoek was excited about his discovery and began to look at other things–saliva from his friend's mouth, sewer water beside his house. In every sample, he found "little animules" and "wee beasties," as he called them. Since no one had ever seen these tiny wiggling creatures before, Van Leeuwenhoek described his findings to a British scientific society.

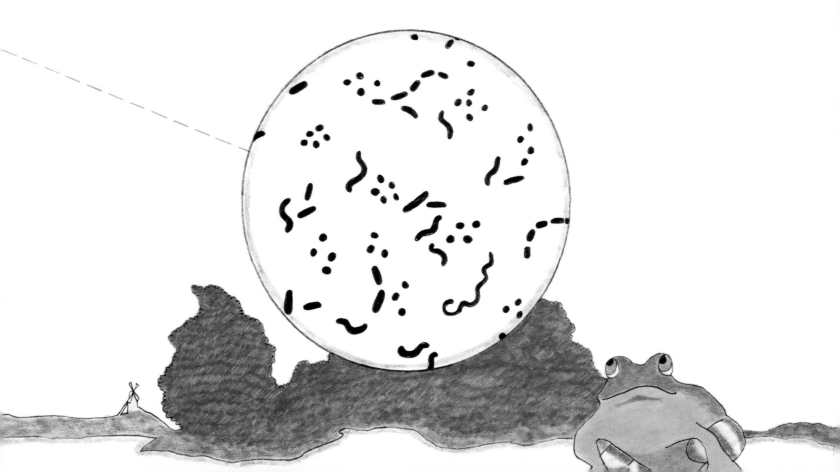

After Van Leeuwenhoek's discovery, scientists began to look at these tiny creatures with better and better magnifying tools. Yet they were puzzled. They knew these tiny creatures were alive by the way they moved. But they didn't know where they came from or what they could do. No one knew that these tiny creatures caused hundreds of familiar changes in the world. Everyday, people saw and smelled and tasted what these small creatures could do. But they did not know it.

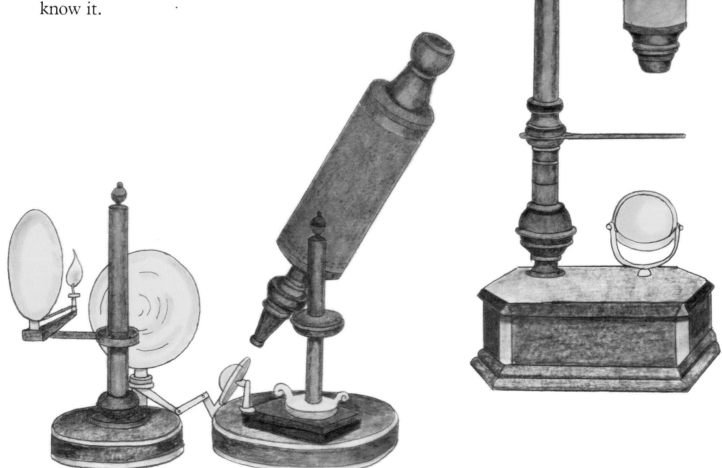

After Van Leeuwenhoek, about two hundred years passed before a famous French scientist, Louis Pasteur, showed how microbes were a part of everyday life. He proved that microbes did not mysteriously arise from dust or soup or dead things, as some people thought. He showed that microbes came from other "parent" microbes and that they traveled through the air on specks of dust. With simple experiments using bottles with crooked necks, he proved that microbes from the air caused soup to spoil and wine to sour. He showed that some microbes were useful and some were harmful.

Today we know a great deal about microbes.

We know that these tiny plants and animals are the smallest forms of life on Earth. We know many different kinds of microbes share our environment. Some make it possible for all other forms of life to exist. Some are harmful, and we try to protect ourselves from these. Still others are useful to us. We have perfected tools to make microbes look larger, so that we can see them,

from the simple hand lens,

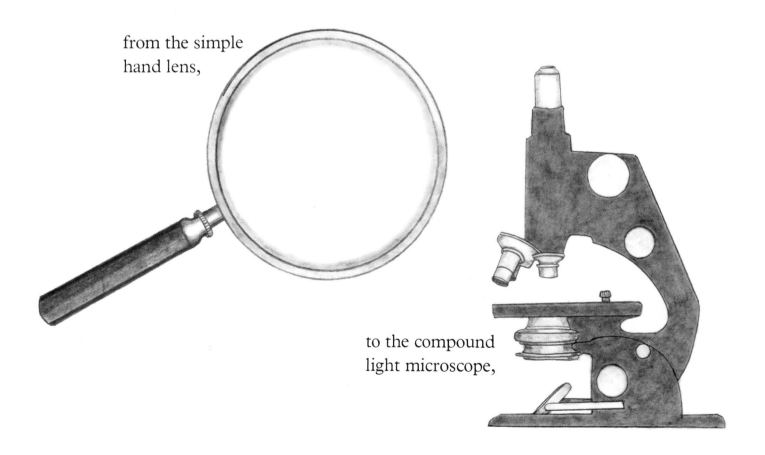

to the compound light microscope,

to the powerful electron microscope
that allows us to see the tiniest ones.

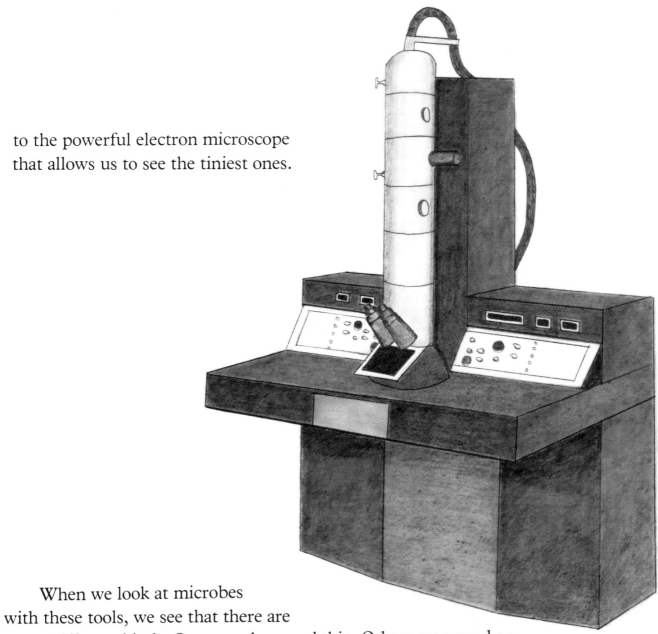

When we look at microbes
with these tools, we see that there are
many different kinds. Some are long and thin. Others are round or
egg-shaped. Some wiggle very fast through a drop of water. Others
just drift slowly along. Some look green or brown, whereas others
seem to have no color at all.

Yet all microbes are alike in one important way. Each microbe is a single cell. A cell is the smallest unit of life. All plants and animals in the world are made up of many cells joined together and working together. Thousands of cells working together form an animal's body —its heart, its bones, its skin or eyes.

In a plant, thousands of cells make up its roots, its leaves, its stems, and its flowers. Cells are different from each other, depending on the job they do. It takes all kinds of cells joined together and working together to make a large living plant or animal.

But microbes are different. Each microbe is just one cell. Each microbe exists all by itself and does not depend on other cells to help it live. Yet, to stay alive, every microbe performs the same important tasks as large plants and animals, made up of many cells. In fact, by studying microbes, we have learned that the basic processes of life are the same for all living things. Anything that is alive must:

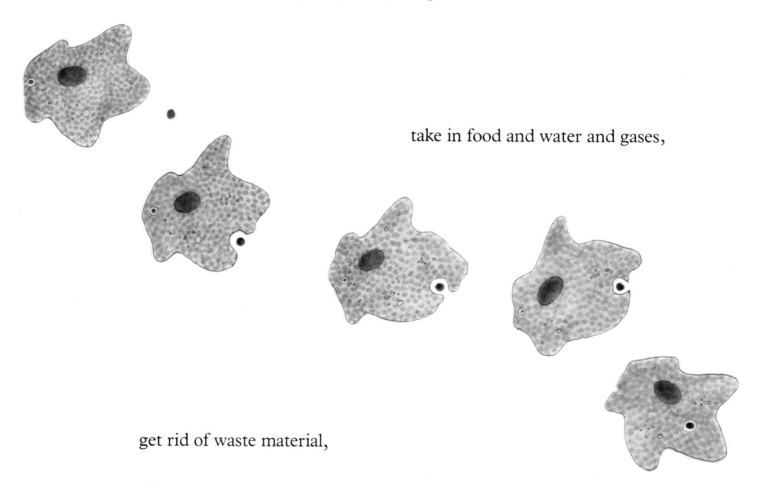

take in food and water and gases,

get rid of waste material,

change when its environment changes, and grow and make more of itself. Each microbe is just one cell, and each microbe does all of these things by itself in order to stay alive.

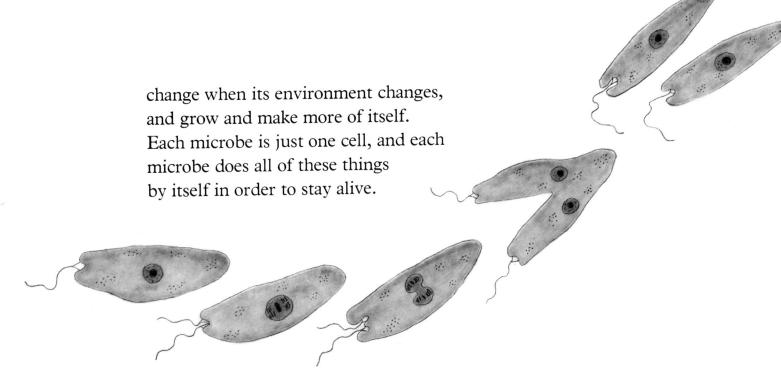

Each kind of microbe grows best under the conditions that are right for it. Some microbes find the right conditions in many places; others grow only in very special places.

Most microbes need oxygen from the air in order to grow. But there are some that grow only where there is no oxygen. These microbes can live deep in the ocean or deep in the soil, or they can even grow inside sealed cans of food. Microbes also need the right temperature. Some grow best where it is very cold, and some grow best where it is very warm. But the largest number of microbes like to grow at a medium temperature, from 20 degrees C (68 degrees F) to 38 degrees C (100 degrees F). These microbes grow well at room temperature. And all microbes grow best in the dark.

The places microbes live give you a clue to the kind of food they need. Microbes that live in the sea find food from fish and water plants. Those that live in swamps are able to find food in the rich mud. Microbes in the soil find food on dead plants and animals. Microbes that live on your skin find food in your dead skin cells and may get moisture from your sweat. Those that live in your intestines use food that you have eaten and that is passing through your body.

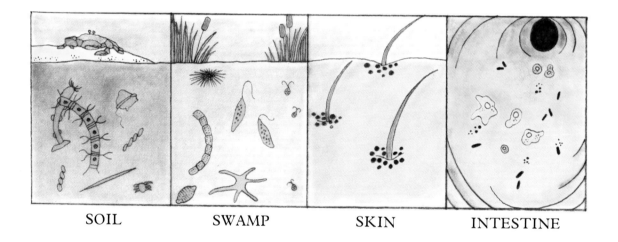

SOIL   SWAMP   SKIN   INTESTINE

No matter where a microbe lives, it must have water to grow. Larger plants and animals die when they cannot find food and water. But not microbes. A few may die, but most just stop growing and wait. They can be blown around by the wind and travel great distances for years. When they finally settle in a place that has water and the right kind of food for them, they will start to grow again.

Some microbes were taken from Egyptian tombs that had been sealed up for 5,000 years. When they were placed on food and water, they started to grow.

When microbes grow, they make more of themselves. If you give microbes all the things they need, they will make more microbes very quickly. Some have a simple way to do this. A single microbe just grows until it is large enough to split in half. It divides, forming 2 microbes just like itself. Then each of these grows and divides again. Now there are 4. Many microbes can do this every twenty minutes. If you started out right now with one microbe on some food, in twenty minutes there would be 2; in forty minutes, 4; and in an hour, 8. In an hour and twenty minutes, there would be 16, and in two hours, there would be 64. In four hours, there would be 5,096. And in one day, there would be billions and billions of microbes—all having started from just one.

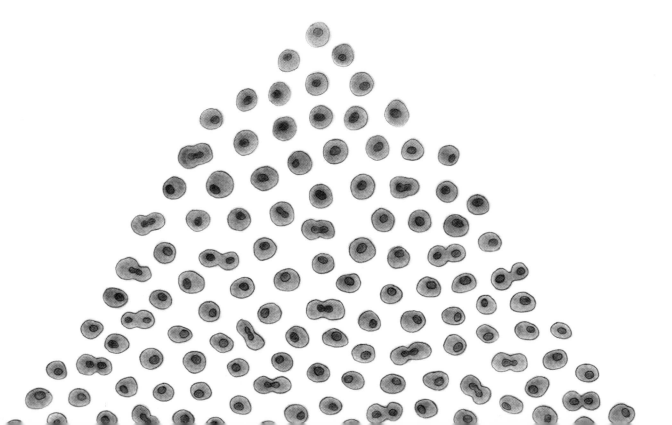

When a large number of microbes are growing together, you can see their growths without magnifying them. They form colorful patches that may look fuzzy or slimy. These growths are called colonies. Each colony started from just one microbe. You have probably seen colonies of microbes growing on many things.

Microbe colonies make:

the green fuzzy growth on lemons and oranges,

the blue-green threads in blue cheese,

the black spots on damp clothing or towels (called mildew),

the yellow or brown spots on flower leaves,

the green scum on top of still ponds,

the slimy greenish stuff on old meat,

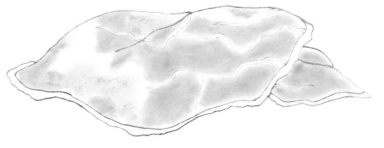

and the gray, brown, or reddish patches on rocks and tree trunks–
these are two different microbes growing together.

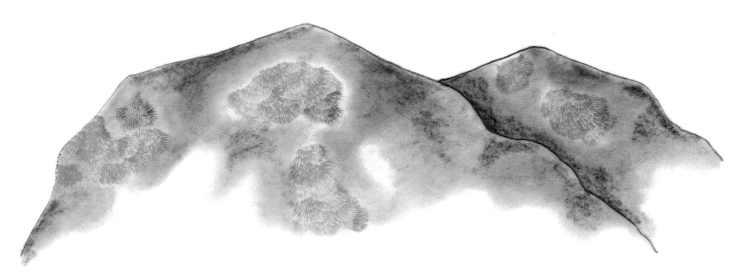

Each of these colonies is made up of millions of one-celled
microbes. They look different because the microbes growing in one
colony are different from the microbes growing in another. Scientists
place microbes into groups and give them special names by looking at
their shape, size, and how and where they grow.

A good way to find out about different microbes is to grow your
own colonies and look at them. Since microbes are almost everyplace
in nature, colonies will grow in a few days, if you just supply food
and water and darkness.

GROW YOUR OWN MICROBES

You Will Need These Things:

a slice of bread or thin slices of a vegetable
    such as a potato, squash, or turnip
cottage cheese in a cardboard container
some dirt
lemon
grass
disposable pie pans, paper towel, plastic wrap,
    clean empty cans, a large glass jar with a cover

What To Do:

Here are four ways you can grow your own microbes.

1. Take a paper towel, and wet it with water. Put the towel in the bottom of the pie pan. Place a slice of bread or some of the vegetable slices on top of the wet towel. Cover the pie pan with plastic wrap, and store it in a dark place like a drawer or cabinet for three days.

2. Cottage cheese usually comes in a cardboard carton. Empty half of the cottage cheese into another container. Sprinkle a little dirt on top of *one* of the cottage cheese samples. Cover both with plastic wrap and store them in a dark place for three days.

3. Put the lemon in an empty can. Add a few drops of water and cover the can tightly with plastic wrap. Store it for one week in a dark place.

4. Take a small handful of grass and put it into a large glass jar. Fill the jar about half full of water, so that the grass is covered. Put the top on the jar, but do not seal it tightly–just a little. Store the jar in a dark place for three days.

CAUTION

Although you won't be growing any harmful microbe colonies, you should be careful when looking at any microbes. Try not to touch the colonies with your hands; if you do, wash your hands with soap and water before you touch anything else. Try not to breathe or blow on the colonies, or you will spread the microbes into the air or get them into your mouth and nose. Don't keep them too long, or they will begin to smell very bad! When you are finished, you can put everything you used into a bag and throw it in the garbage.

What To Look For:

1. Bread or vegetable slice

After three days look at the bread or vegetable slices. Do you see thin threads spreading over the surface? This is a *mold* growing. Notice how the threads spread out and twist in all directions, forming a soft web. With a hand lens, you can see that some of the threads may have little dark round sacs on them. These sacs are the holders for tiny grains called spores. Spores are the mold's way of making new cells. When spores are spread by the wind or by insects and carried to some damp food, they open and a new thread starts to grow. As it grows longer, it branches out into more and more threads. Soon the threads tangle, and a whole new mold colony is formed.

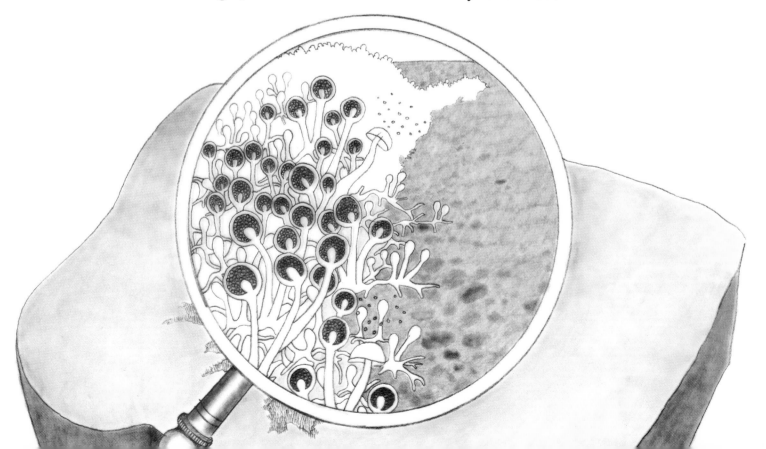

2. Cottage cheese

Look at the cottage cheese. Both containers should have colonies growing on top. But the one with the dirt added should have many more, because dirt has lots of different microbes in it. Are there fuzzy-looking colonies growing? These are also molds, but different from the ones that grew on the bread and vegetable slices. Do you see any soft, slimy-looking colonies that are yellow, orange, or white? This is another type of microbe growing. They are called *yeasts*. One yeast cell is very small, but you can just see it using a hand lens. A yeast cell is shaped like an egg. Some may have little bumps, or "buds," on their sides. This is the way new yeast cells are made. The buds just grow bigger and finally break away—a new yeast cell!

Look at the cottage cheese a little more carefully. Do you see any smaller colonies that are yellow, cream-colored, or red? You may also have colonies like these on the vegetable slices. They look shiny and moist. The microbes growing in these colonies are the smallest plants in the world. They are called *bacteria*. You cannot see them without a microscope. If you did see them magnified, you would notice that bacteria have different shapes. Some are round; others are shaped like a little rod or stick; still others are spiral, like a spring.

3. Lemon
Look at the lemon. It will probably
have another kind of mold growing on it.
This mold is green and very soft. It has been named
Penicillium. It is the same kind of mold you can see growing in
blue cheese and the one from which an important medicine,
penicillin, is made.

4. Grass water

Look at the jar of grass water. The water was clear three days ago.
Now it is cloudy, because millions of microbes that were living on
the grass have started to grow. Does the water smell bad? That tells
you microbes are growing and giving off waste materials. In this water
you could find all kinds of microbes, but especially the tiny green
plant microbes called *algae* and the one-celled animals called *protozoa.*
Algae are one-celled green plants. Like bigger green plants, they trap
energy from the sun to make sugar and release oxygen into the air.
We breathe this oxygen and could not live without it. Algae are the
biggest of all microbes and are easy to see with a hand lens.

Protozoa are the smallest animals in the world. They do not look like any animals you have seen. If you looked at a drop of the grass water under a microscope, you might see some protozoa that are small globs of colorless jelly stuff. They move just by oozing along. Or you might see some that have little hairs all over their bodies. These hairs beat very fast and make the tiny animals move. Still others have long whiplike parts that wave back and forth. Protozoa are part of the great cycle of food in nature. They are the first food for baby fish. Larger fish eat the baby fish, and they in turn are eaten by man.

Long before people knew microbes existed, they learned how to use the changes microbes make. The Bible tells of making wine out of the juice pressed from grapes. Back then, people didn't know it was yeasts growing on the grapes that changed sugar into alcohol and turned the grape juice into wine. A long time ago, people who baked bread learned that if they used a little bit of special dough, their bread would be light and fluffy, instead of flat like a pancake. They didn't know it was yeasts in the special dough that made the bread light.

Today we use microbes to make lots of things.
Microbes help make:

the bubbles in root beer,
the sour taste of pickles and sauerkraut,
the vitamins you take,
medicines, cheeses, and yogurt,
rich and fertile soil.

Just by living and growing, by taking in food that they need and expelling what they do not need, microbes change their surroundings —and ours. In the process of living, microbes make powerful chemicals that help change the food they are using and the air around them. Often, we can see and smell and taste these changes. We take advantage of some of the changes to make foods we like and medicines we need. Here are three easy projects you can do to see how living microbes make things change.

CURDS AND WHEY

The milk that comes directly from the cow already has many microbes in it. But the milk we drink has been pasteurized, or heated, until most of the microbes, especially the harmful ones, have been killed. Yet some remain alive. If these are allowed to grow, they will cause changes in the milk, which you can see.

You Will Need These Things:

> 1/2 pint of fresh milk
> a little bit of soil
> four clear glass baby food jars
> with covers

What To Do:

Pour an equal amount of milk into
the four baby food jars and put a
number on each jar.
Cover jar 1 tightly and put it in the
refrigerator.

Cover jar 2 tightly and store it at room
temperature in a dark place.

Do not cover jar 3. Store it at room
temperature in a dark place.

Add a small bit of soil to jar 4; cover
it and store at room temperature
in a dark place.

What To Look For:

After five days, line up all the jars and look at them. Jar 1 should look the same. Smell it. Does it smell sweet or sour? Cold slows down the growth of most microbes, so this jar will show the smallest change.

Jar 2 may have a small separation. Look for a thick layer at the bottom of the jar. This is a curd. There should be a thin, watery layer at the top. This is whey. At room temperature, the microbes in the milk began to grow. They made powerful chemicals that changed the natural sugar in the milk into acid. Smell the milk. Does it smell sour? The acid caused the milk to separate into curds and whey.

Jar 3 should also have a slightly larger curd at the bottom. Since it was left open to the air, some microbes may have fallen into the milk and started to grow. In the dairy industry, microbes are used to sour milk so that a curd will form. The curd is the start of all cheeses. Plain curd is cottage cheese. Other cheeses are made by squeezing curds into solid blocks and then adding special microbes to give different smells and flavors. There are holes in Swiss cheese because the microbes that flavor Swiss cheese release gases. The gases get trapped in the curd, forming gas pockets, or holes, in the cheese.

Jar 4 should have a big solid curd at the bottom. This jar will also have a strong sour smell. The milk in this jar is the most changed, because you added many more microbes when you added the dirt.

YEAST AND DOUGH

You Will Need These Things:

one cup flour, one tablespoon sugar, one package
    of dried baker's yeast (from the store)
1/4 cup of warm water
a tall glass jar

What To Do:

1. Add the yeast to the warm water. Put the flour into the glass jar. Slowly add the yeast mixture to the flour in the jar, stirring with a spoon until a sticky dough is formed. Push the dough down into the bottom of the jar and mark the level of the dough on the outside of the jar.

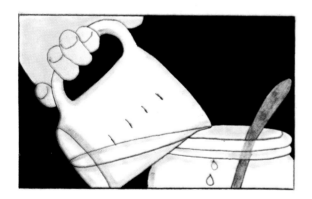

2. Put the jar in a warm place—a pot of warm water is fine. Every ten minutes take the jar out and make a mark by the height of the dough. Stop after an hour.

What To Look For:

The dough should have risen for the first thirty to forty minutes and then stopped. The yeasts are growing and changing the starch in the flour into gases and other chemicals. Because the dough is sticky, the gases get trapped. The dough stretched around the gas—just as a balloon stretches when you blow it up. This is why the dough rises. The gas "blows" the dough up. Do you see any big gas bubbles? They form when lots of yeast cells grow in one place. All over the world, yeasts are used in bread dough to make it rise.

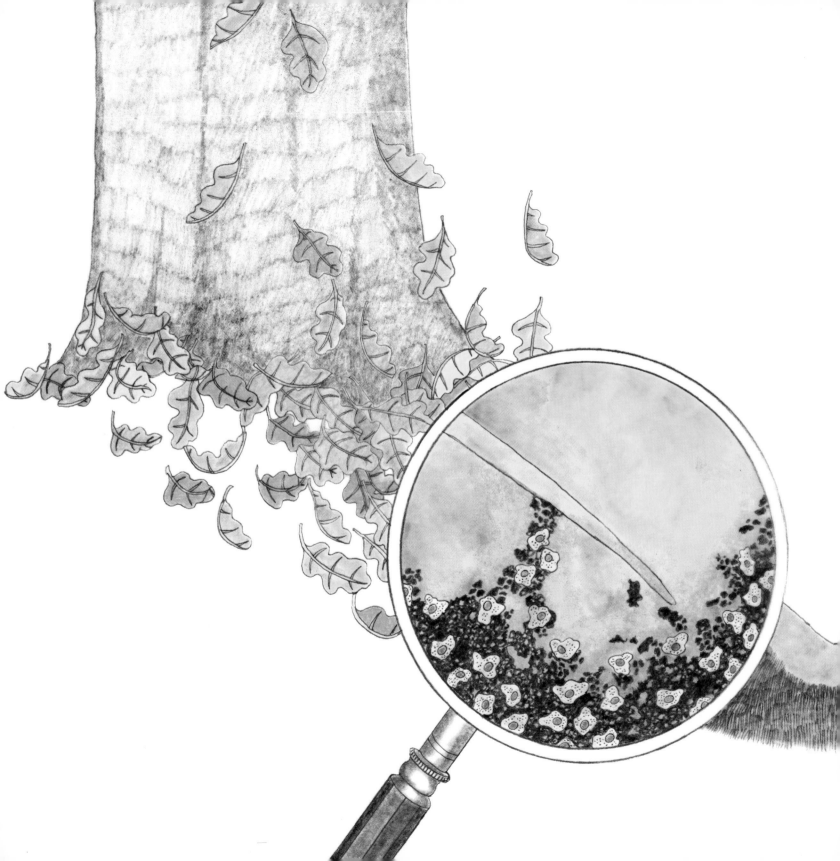

MICROBES IN NATURE

Microbes are nature's recyclers. When something dies, microbes start to use the dead material as food for their own growth. The process is called decay. It is the way dead things disappear from our world, so that new things can grow. Leaves that fall from the trees in autumn are decayed by microbes in the soil. Rain provides the water. The leaves turn dark and crumble apart because the microbes are breaking down the large chemicals in the leaves and changing them into smaller and simpler materials. In the spring, new plants use these simple materials for their growth. If microbes did not cause decay, every living thing that died would pile up on the earth's surface. By breaking down dead material into simple substances that return to the air and soil, microbes make it possible for all other forms of life to exist. You can do an experiment to see microbes cause decay.

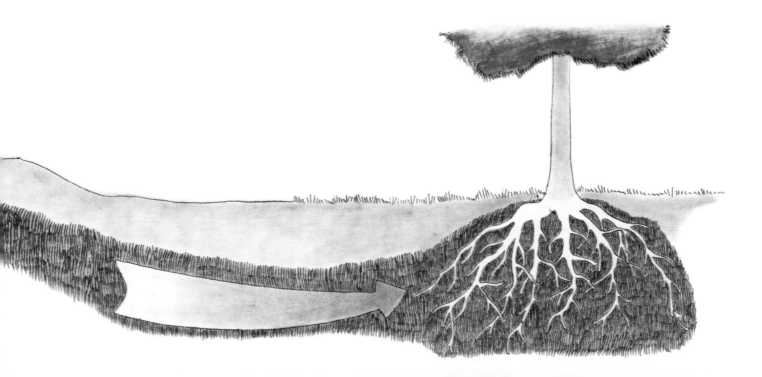

You Will Need These Things:

grass clippings and leaves (fresh and green)
glass jar with a lid
a few drops of water

What To Do:

Pack the grass clippings and leaves
tightly until the jar is about one-half
full. Sprinkle a few drops of water on
top. Put the lid on, but do not put it on
tightly. (If the lid is on tightly, the
gases given off will make the jar break!)
Place the jar in a dark, warm place and
look at it every two days.

What To Look For:

Watch for these changes. It may take a month for this test to be
completed.

Juices from the grass and leaves will begin to collect first. Microbes
grow in these juices, and the juice will become cloudy. The mixture
will pack down and become smelly. After a few weeks the mixture
will be dark brown, and you won't be able to see any green grass or
leaves. In nature, these substances return to the soil to make it rich
and fertile.

Sometimes the changes microbes make as they live and grow are not good for us. So, to protect ourselves from harmful microbes, we have learned to control the growth of microbes. There are easy ways to do this. Since microbes cannot grow without water, foods can be dried to keep microbes from growing on them. Cold slows down the growth of many microbes, so we put our food in the refrigerator or freezer to keep it fresh. High temperatures kill microbes, so water that has been boiled and well-cooked foods are safe to eat. The microbes on our skin and hair get washed away with soap and water. Iodine or alcohol placed on a cut will keep microbes out. When we get sick, we can take medicines that help our bodies fight the microbes causing the disease.

But most often, the changes microbes make do not hurt us. In fact, as you have seen, we use microbes to help make some of the food we eat. We eat those microbes right along with our food!

There are millions and millions of microbes around us, silently growing every minute of every day. It is hard to believe that these invisible bits of life cause so many changes we use and depend upon. Microbes are as alive as we are. They may be unseen, but they are mighty.